FACT or FICTION?

DO ALIENS EXIST?

PETER FINN

Gareth Stevens PUBLISHING

Please visit our website, www.garethstevens.com. For a free color catalog of all our high-quality books, call toll free 1-800-542-2595 or fax 1-877-542-2596.

Library of Congress Cataloging-in-Publication Data
Names: Finn, Peter, 1978- author.
Title: Do aliens exist? / Peter Finn.
Description: New York : Gareth Stevens Publishing, [2023] | Series: Fact or fiction? | Includes index.
Identifiers: LCCN 2021055113 (print) | LCCN 2021055114 (ebook) | ISBN 9781538280690 (Library Binding) | ISBN 9781538280676 (Paperback) | ISBN 9781538280683 (Set) | ISBN 9781538280706 (eBook)
Subjects: LCSH: Extraterrestrial beings–Juvenile literature. | Unidentified flying objects–Juvenile literature.
Classification: LCC QB54 .F445 2023 (print) | LCC QB54 (ebook) | DDC 576.8/39–dc23/eng/20211223
LC record available at https://lccn.loc.gov/2021055113
LC ebook record available at https://lccn.loc.gov/2021055114

Published in 2023 by
Gareth Stevens Publishing
29 E. 21st Street
New York, NY 10010

Designer: Sheryl Kober
Editor: Therese Shea

Photo credits: Cover (top) and p. 1 solarseven/Shutterstock.com; cover and p. 1 (bottom image) LenaGraphics/Shutterstock.com; pp. 1-32 (background texture) Olga Korica/Shutterstock.com; pp. 1-32 (sidebar background texture) leolintang/Shutterstock.com; back cover and pp. 2-32 (It's A Fact background texture) Olga Korica/Shutterstock.com; p. 3 Tithi Luadthong/Shutterstock.com; p. 4 DEL Studio/Shutterstock.com; p. 5 (top) Fotokita/Shutterstock.com; p. 5 (bottom) adike/Shutterstock.com; p. 6 Vorobiov Oleksii 8/Shutterstock.com; p. 7 (top) javarman/Shutterstock.com; p. 7 (bottom) f11photo/Shutterstock.com; p. 8 Yeti Crab / Shutterstock.com; p. 9 (top) Dimitrios Karamitros/Shutterstock.com; p. 9 (bottom) mari2d/Shutterstock.com; p. 10 lassedesignen/Shutterstock.com; p. 11 (top) Nikta_Nikta/Shutterstock.com; p. 11 (middle) Public Domain, https://commons.wikimedia.org/w/index.php?curid=200531; p. 10 (bottom) 3 AleksB59 /Shutterstock.com; p. 12 selivanoff1986/Shutterstock.com; p. 13 (top) ktsdesign / Shutterstock.com; p. 13 (bottom) https://en.wikipedia.org/wiki/Roswell_incident#/media/File:RoswellDailyRecordJuly8,1947.jpg; p. 14 selivanoff1986/Shutterstock.com; p. 15 (top) Traveller70/Shutterstock.com; p. 15 (bottom right) https://commons.wikimedia.org/wiki/File:Marcel-roswell-debris_0.jpg; p. 15 (bottom left) GabrielJose/Shutterstock.com; p. 16 Natalia Sedyakina/Shutterstock.com; p. 17 (top) garykingphotographer/Shutterstock.com; p. 17 (bottom) ehrlif/Shutterstock.com; p. 18 Alexander_P/Shutterstock.com; p. 19 (top) https://en.wikipedia.org/wiki/Boeing_F/A-18E/F_Super_Hornet#/media/File:US_Navy_071203-N-8923M-074_An_F-A-18F_Super_Hornet,_from_the_Red_Rippers_of_Strike_Fighter_Squadron_(VFA)_11,_makes_a_sharp_turn_above_the_flight_deck_aboard_the_Nimitz-class_nuclear-powered_aircraft_carrier_USS_Harry_S._Truman.jpg%20or%20https://en.wikipedia.org/wiki/Boeing_F/A-18E/F_Super_Hornet#/media/File:Four_Super_Hornets.jpg; p. 19 (bottom) lassedesignen/Shutterstock.com; p. 20 Morphart Creation/Shutterstock.com; p. 21 (top) Guillermo Caffarini/Shutterstock.com; p. 21 (bottom) Nicolai Solbakk Willumsen/Shutterstock.com; p. 22 Barmaleeva/Shutterstock.com; p. 23 (top) Dmitry Kalinovsky/Shutterstock.com; p. 23 (bottom, left to right) https://en.wikipedia.org/wiki/The_War_of_the_Worlds#/media/File:War_of_the_Worlds_original_cover_bw.jpg, https://en.wikipedia.org/wiki/The_War_of_the_Worlds#/media/File:War_of_the_Worlds_original_cover_bw.jpg, https://en.wikipedia.org/wiki/The_War_of_the_Worlds_(1938_radio_drama)#/media/File:Landingsite_statue.JPG; p. 24 (top) Agor2012/Shutterstock.com; p. 24 (bottom left) DanieleGay/Shutterstock.com; p. 25 (top) John A Davis/Shutterstock.com; p. 25 (bottom) https://upload.wikimedia.org/wikipedia/commons/7/78/Niac2020_bandyopadhyay.jpg; p. 26 Marta Leo/Shutterstock.com; p. 27 (top) https://commons.wikimedia.org/wiki/File:Arecibo_radio_telescope_SJU_06_2019_6144.jpg; p. 27 (bottom) Joseph Sohm/Shutterstock.com; p. 29 GabrielJose/Shutterstock.com; p. 29 GabrielJose/Shutterstock.com and Space creator/Shutterstock.com

Printed in the United States of America

CPSIA compliance information: Batch #CSGS23: For further information contact Gareth Stevens, New York, New York, at 1-800-542-2595.

CONTENTS

Words in the glossary appear in **bold** type the first time they are used in the text.

IS ANYONE OUT THERE?

Earth is home to millions of animal and plant species. From its deepest oceans to its highest mountains, it's filled with life. More than 7.5 billion people live on our planet!

In our solar system, Earth is the only planet that supports life. Scientists have found no other planets that have any form of life so far. However, some people think there must be life on other planets outside our solar system. Some even think these living creatures may be able to communicate with humans. We call these beings aliens.

The word "alien" means someone who's not from a certain place. Another name for a life-form not from Earth is "extraterrestrial." Many people tell stories about extraterrestrials coming to Earth. Are they true?

ARE WE ALONE?

In some stories, aliens land on Earth to learn about humans and share what they know. In other tales, these creatures come to take over Earth and destroy humans. Most scientists don't think aliens have come to Earth yet. But there are people who disagree. They think aliens have been landing on Earth for a long time and it's bad luck that there's so little evidence—or that the evidence has been hidden on purpose.

There are at least 100 billion stars just in our galaxy, which is called the Milky Way (above). Each star has at least one planet. Is one of those planets home to alien life?

IT'S A FACT!

As of 2021, more than 4,000 exoplanets, or planets outside Earth's solar system, have been discovered.

ALIEN ARTISTS AND ARCHITECTS?

Some think aliens helped people create a few amazing sites long ago. This is called the "ancient alien theory." Believers in this idea point to cave paintings in Australia and some Egyptian **hieroglyphs** that look like aliens. The stone heads on Easter Island and even the Egyptian pyramids have been credited to aliens as well. However, most evidence shows humans alone created these marvels.

The Nazca Lines of Peru cover about 170 square miles (440 square km). When the designs were spotted from the air, some thought aliens created them as spaceship runways. Most archaeologists, however, maintain that the over 2,000-year-old drawings were shaped by the Nazca and Paracas people of the region. They don't believe in the ancient alien theory.

ALIEN APPEARANCES

No one can agree about how aliens from another planet might look. Science fiction has made us picture extraterrestrial life a bit like us but with a slightly odd appearance. Some imagine aliens as short with green skin. Others say they'd have large heads and gray skin. Still others picture them with black eyes and long fingers. Or maybe they would be tall and thin? Aliens could look more like bugs or some other kind of creature too!

Easter Island

Sometimes the ancient alien theory is called the ancient astronaut theory. Do you think this prehistoric rock drawing in Peru (above) looks like an ancient alien?

IT'S A FACT!

Easter Island—located in the Pacific Ocean, west of Chile—is home to about 900 stone statues with large heads. Most people don't think aliens created them.

MESSAGES FROM EARTH

Voyager 1 and 2 are two probes, or unmanned machines meant to gather information about space, that were launched in 1977 to the planets of the outer solar system. Both probes have transmitted details about Jupiter, Saturn, Uranus, and Neptune. But that's not the probes' only purpose. Each spacecraft is carrying messages on a Golden Record, just in case they encounter intelligent extraterrestrial life.

Carl Sagan

The Golden Records are 12-inch (30.5 cm) gold-plated copper disks with images and recordings meant to tell aliens about humans and other life on Earth. They contain sounds like heartbeats, laughter, and a kiss between mother and child. They also include music, such as that of the classical genius Ludwig van Beethoven and rock-and-roll pioneer Chuck Berry. Symbols show how the record can be played.

THE GOLDEN RECORDS

So, who decided what was included on the Golden Records to introduce all of humankind to aliens? A group led by famous American astronomer Carl Sagan chose their contents for NASA (National Aeronautics and Space Administration). The group selected 115 images of Earth as well as sounds of nature, such as thunder, birds, and whales. They also included greetings in 55 languages in addition to a message from U.S. president Jimmy Carter.

ALIENS in EARTH ENTERTAINMENT

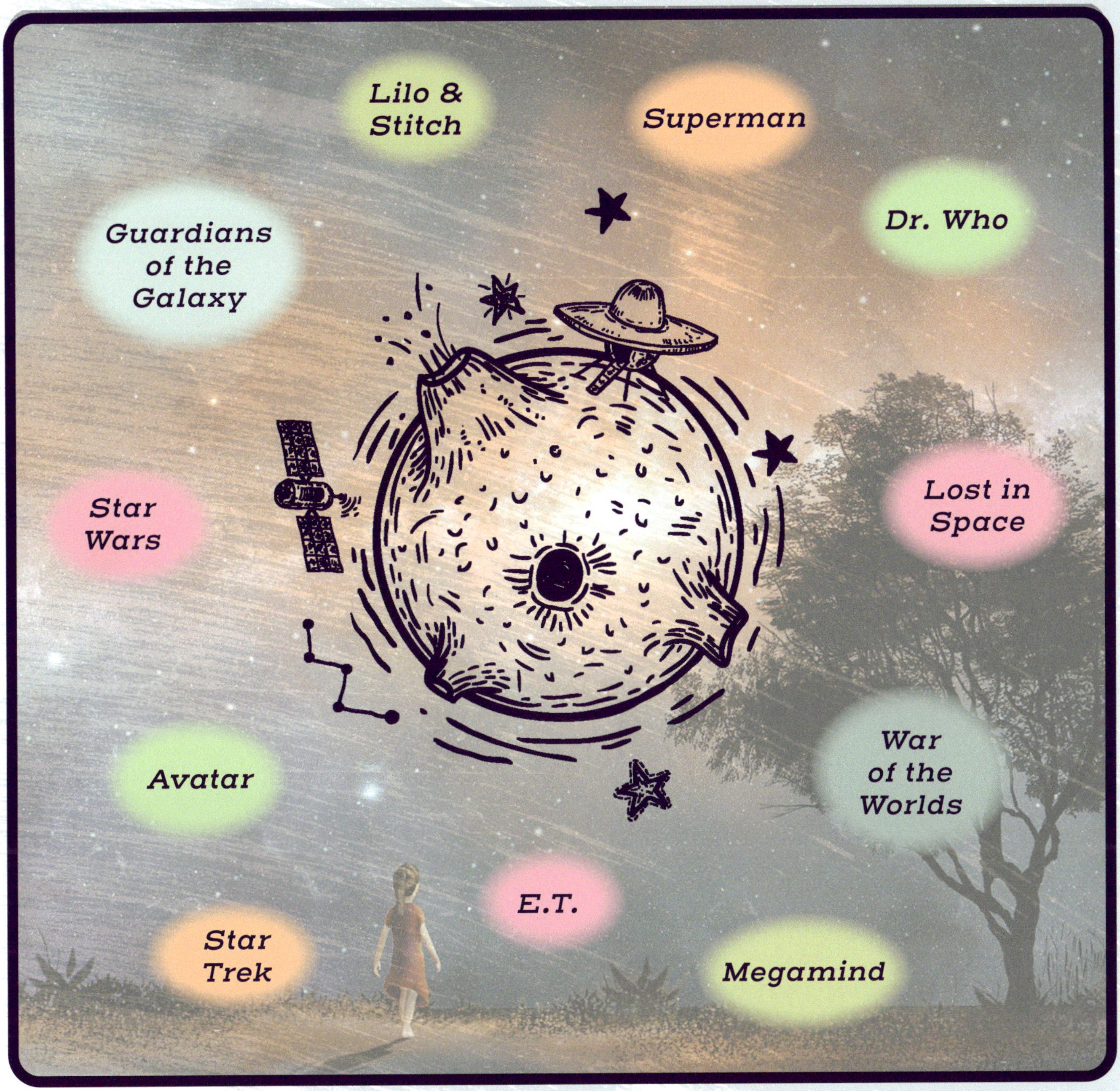

Aliens inspire much popular fiction. Some of Earth's most famous aliens are featured in movies and TV shows.

IT'S A FACT!

The National U.F.O. Reporting Center announced that more than 7,200 UFO sightings were reported in the United States in 2020 alone.

GLOSSARY

abduct: to take away by force

autopsy: an examination of a dead body with the aim of discovering a cause of death

conspiracy: a secret plan made by two or more people to carry out something that may be harmful or illegal

electromagnetic: the magnetic field that a current of electricity produces

hallucination: something that is seen but isn't actually there

hieroglyph: an ancient form of writing made of small images

Pentagon: the headquarters of the U.S. Department of Defense located in Washington, D.C. Also, the military leaders that work there.

phenomenon: something unusual or difficult to understand or explain fully that can be seen and studied. The plural is phenomena.

rover: a vehicle created to explore the surface of a moon or planet

skeptical: having doubt about something

squadron: a division of military organization, smaller than a unit but larger than a platoon

technology: using science, engineering, and other industries to invent useful tools or to solve problems. Also, a machine, piece of equipment, or method created by technology.

FOR MORE INFORMATION

BOOKS

Hile, Lori. *Aliens and UFOs: Myth or Reality?* North Mankato, MN: Capstone Press, 2019.

Kallen, Stuart A. *Do Aliens Exist?* San Diego, CA: ReferencePoint Press, Inc., 2016.

Murray, Laura K. *Aliens.* Mankato, MN: Creative Education/Creative Paperbacks, 2017.

WEBSITES

Mars 2020 Mission Perseverance Rover: Quick Facts
mars.nasa.gov/mars2020/
Discover what the Perseverance rover is exploring on Mars.

SETI Institute
www.seti.org/
See what strides this organization is making in the search for extraterrestrial life.

We Asked a NASA Scientist: Do Aliens Exist?
www.nasa.gov/feature/episode-5-we-asked-a-nasa-scientist-do-aliens-exist
Find out what the experts say!

Publisher's note to educators and parents: Our editors have carefully reviewed these websites to ensure that they are suitable for students. Many websites change frequently, however, and we cannot guarantee that a site's future contents will continue to meet our high standards and educational value. Be advised that students should be closely supervised whenever they access the internet.

INDEX